A TASTE OF DURAZZANO

A TASTE OF DURAZZANO

A COOKBOOK FROM OLD FAMILY RECIPES AND SOME NEW ONES

ELIZABETH IADEVAIA

iUniverse, Inc.
New York   Bloomington

iUniverse books may be ordered through booksellers or by contacting:

iUniverse
1663 Liberty Drive
Bloomington, IN 47403
www.iuniverse.com
1-800-Authors (1-800-288-4677)

Because of the dynamic nature of the Internet, any Web addresses or links contained in this book may have changed since publication and may no longer be valid. The views expressed in this work are solely those of the author and do not necessarily reflect the views of the publisher, and the publisher hereby disclaims any responsibility for them.

ISBN: 978-1-4401-2462-4 (sc)
ISBN: 978-1-4401-2461-7 (ebook)

Printed in the United States of America

iUniverse rev. date: 07/16/09

INTRODUCTION

Happy times are always shared with food and families.
Memories and story telling allow our children to understand
and share our heritage. New memories and old ones tell the
stories of our lives. Food always made us feel better, or at
least helped.

ALS robbed my family of a lifetime of new memories. ALS
ended life for my husband, Camillo and robbed my children
of many more years with their dad. Family was the core of
life according to Camillo. We will forever miss his presence
and sense of humor, but he will always be in our hearts. As
the disease progressed, my husband was unable to chew and
swallow his food but I would puree the same food prepared
for all and feed him thru his feeding tube. In our case food
was shared in happy and not so happy times, but we were
still together and sharing.

This must be a sad way to introduce a cookbook, but in spite of the many years of sadness and
grief, we did not allow this awful disease of ALS to stop us from living. Together we still had
family gatherings and celebrations for our children; Holy Communion, Confirmation, holidays
and birthdays. Writing this book allowed me to remember all the happy times we shared in
our short life together.

ACKNOWLEDGMENTS

This book would not have been possible without the inspiration of my late husband, Camillo. I wish he could be beside me as I turn the pages. He lost his life at age 47 to a long battle with ALS (Lou Gering's disease) but we shared a passion for simple cooking and love for each other. The many memories we shared in our almost 16 years of marriage gave me the encouragement to record all these wonderful recipes our families have shared for more than 100 years. We were both born in a small town in Italy named Durazzano. I at age 12 and he at

15 immigrated to America with our families and years later met and married. Our roots were the same and so was our passion for our heritage and culture. So, here I am wanting to share just a piece of it with my children and their families to come.

To my mother Teresa at age 81, thank you for having taught me all that I know about food and family. Thanks for clearing up some old time recipes to write in my book.

To my sister, Filomena, thank you for coming over many nights to test and retest some old recipes and to check for accurate measurements. Also, thank you for the support and love we share.

To Vincent and Cathryn, you are the love of my life. Thanks for all your help on the computer to make this book possible.

CONTENTS

APPETIZERS, SIDE DISHES, AND VEGETABLES

1

TORTA DI SPINACI

Spinach Quiche or Broccoli Quiche

1 Pastry crust (homemade or store bought)
1 small onion chopped
1- 8oz package chopped frozen spinach (defrost) or chopped broccoli
3 beaten eggs
1-cup plain yogurt
½ cup milk
Salt and pepper to taste
½ cup shredded cheddar cheese
½ cup shredded mozzarella cheese
2 tablespoons Parmesan cheese

Drain and squeeze excess water from spinach
Mix all ingredients
Place pastry crust into a 9–inch quiche dish. Pour in mixture
Bake 350-degree oven for 45 minutes. Remove and cool
Serve warm

BRUSCHETTA

Tomatoes 2 large or 3-4 medium any variety
Day Old Italian bread sliced and lightly toasted (peasant bread works great also)
4-5 fresh basil leaves chopped
1 clove chopped garlic
2 tablespoons extra virgin olive oil
1 teaspoon dried oregano

1-teaspoon kosher salt
Mix all the above ingredients. Let it sit for 10-15 then spoon on toasted bread.
Serves 6-8 people

PEPERONI IMBOTTITI

Stuffed Italian Peppers

8-12 medium long green Italian peppers
2-3 fillet anchovies
1-tablespoon capers in vinegar
2 large slices day Old Italian bread soaked in water. Squeeze excess water and crumble
Pepper and salt to taste
1 lightly beaten egg
1 teaspoon red wine vinegar
5 tablespoon of extra virgin olive oil
1 teaspoon dried oregano
2 tablespoon of chopped Gaeta olives or calamata

Hollow peppers remove seeds and stem
Wash and dry well
Mix all ingredients (reserve half of oil for frying later)
Stuff pepper
On medium heat, place 2 tablespoon of oil in a large non-stick skillet.
Let oil heat, and then place the stuffed pepper with stuffed part down into the skillet. Let cook until a crust has formed then lay them down. Cook on all sides until lightly golden. Remove and place on paper towel to drain. Transfer to a platter and serve hot.

MELENZANE IMBOTTITE

Stuffed Baby Italian Eggplants

4-6 medium eggplants
2 large slices day Old Italian bread soaked in water and crumbled (squeeze out excess water)
2 peeled chopped tomatoes
2 eggs lightly beaten
Salt and pepper to taste
1 garlic clove chopped
2-tablespoon Parmesan cheese
Fresh basil chopped (4-5 leaves)
1 teaspoon dried oregano

2-4 tablespoon of extra virgin olive oil

Roll eggplant to soften the flesh inside.

Slice in half lengthwise

Remove flesh and reserve skin to fill later.

Chop the flesh and sauté in pan with 2 tablespoon of olive oil. Add the rest of the ingredients

Stuff the hollow halved eggplant with the mixture

Fry in pan upside down until crust forms (use the remaining olive oil for frying)

Transfer to baking dish and bake for 45 minutes in a 325-degree oven.

Remove from oven. Plain tomato sauce (recipe in the book) should be served on top of cooked eggplant.

ZUCCHINI E MELENZANE ARROSTITE

Grilled Zucchini and Eggplant

3-4 medium zucchini

2 medium eggplants or 4 baby eggplants

3-5 tablespoon extra virgin olive oil

1-2 teaspoon kosher salt

1 clove garlic finely chopped

1/4-teaspoon red pepper flakes (optional)

2-tablespoon balsamic vinegar

4-5 leaves fresh basil (rough chop)

1-tablespoon fresh thyme

Serves 6-8 people

Slice the vegetables about 1/4 of inch thick; sprinkle some salt and a little oil. Place on hot grill

Cook turning once for about 3 minutes on each side. Transfer to platter and add remaining ingredients.

PEPERONI ARROSTITI

Grilled Peppers

4-5 large red bell peppers (other colors can be added or substituted)
Wash and dry
Place on a grill and allow the skin to burn, turn several times
Peel charred skin
Remove seeds, do not wash. Slice in half or in long strips
2 cloves chopped garlic
1 teaspoon kosher or sea salt
2-tablespoon balsamic vinegar
4 tablespoon of extra virgin olive oil
1-teaspoon fresh thyme
1-teaspoon fresh Italian parsley

Add the above ingredients to sliced peppers. Serve at room temperature

PIZZELLE FIOR DI ZUCCHINI

Zucchini Flower Dumpling

2 Cups vegetable oil
2 Cups all purpose unbleached flour
1 Tablespoon kosher salt
1 Tablespoon black pepper
1 Teaspoon baking powder
1 Egg
2 Tablespoon Parmesan cheese

1/2 Cup or more of blanched Zucchini Flowers (purchase at local market or grow them in the garden.)
    Place washed zucchini flower in salted boiling water for about 5 minutes.
Drain and set aside
1/4 Cup or more of iced water

In large bowl place flour, salt, baking powder, cheese and pepper, add the egg and a little iced water. Mix well with a fork. Add more water if needed. The mixture should be like soft pizza dough. Mix in the blanched zucchini flowers (available only in early summer).

In a large non-stick skillet place 1 cup of vegetable oil and heat. Carefully drop 1 tablespoon full of the mixture into the hot oil. Several will fit into the skillet. Continue to cook them on medium heat until golden, turn and cook the other side, turning only once. Repeat until all is done. You may need to add the rest of the oil as you continue. Serve them hot.

These little pizzelle can be made with other blanched vegetables, like cauliflowers, broccoli or mushrooms.

BROCCOLI DI RAPE

Broccoli di Rabe

2 bunches of broccoli rabe
2-tablespoon kosher salt
1 chopped garlic clove
1/4 cup of extra virgin olive oil
4 or more quarts of water

Clean and wash the broccoli rabe. Remove the tough leaves and tough stems. Bring water to boil, add salt and drop the broccoli rabe, cook until stems are tender. Place in a serving platter; add garlic, olive oil and more salt if necessary. Serve as a side dish

ANTIPASTO

1/2 Lb. of prosciutto sliced thin or in strips
1 dry sweet sausage sliced thin
1/2 lb. of capicolla sliced thin
1 lb. of provolone auricchio sharp cut in wedges
1 lb. of Gaeta olives or use your favorite ones
1 small jar of anchovies fillets in oil
1 tablespoon of capers in vinegar (drained)
1 jar of giardiniera (homemade or store bought) Pickled vegetables
1 cup picked hot or sweet peppers seeded and sliced (optional or if available) recipe in the book
1/4 cup of extra virgin olive oil
1 teaspoon of dried oregano
Black pepper (optional).

In a large oval platter arrange prosciutto, sausage and capicolla on one side and on the other side place your sliced wedges of cheese. In a separate platter, place rinsed giardiniera, pickled sliced peppers. Take each anchovy and roll one olive around and arrange over the vegetable platter. Sprinkle in the capers and rest of olives. Add the extra virgin olive oil over the vegetable platter. Serve crusty Italian bread with these two wonderful platters. This antipasto is always served before a big meal on holidays. Black cracked pepper and be added over the meats. Serves 6-8 people

INSALATA DI MARE

Seafood Salad (Served on Christmas Eve)

2 lbs of cleaned calamari (both tails and body)
1 lb. of cleaned medium shrimps (leave tail on)
½ lb. of sea scallops
1/4 cup of fresh Italian parsley
2-3 chopped garlic cloves
1/4 cup of extra virgin olive oil
Kosher salt (about 1 teaspoon)

Pepper to taste
Juice of one lemon
1 lemon cut in wedges for garnish
2 chopped celery stalks in bites

Boil a large pot of water. Drop the cleaned uncut calamari, and cook approximately 15 minutes or until fork tender. Drain and set aside. Repeat with boiling water for shrimp and scallops. Cook for 5-6 minutes. Drain and set aside. Cut the calamari into ring about 1/8 thick. Toss in boiled shrimps and scallops. Add garlic, oil, lemon juice, salt, pepper and celery. Toss and taste. More salt and pepper can be added if needed. Add parsley. Do not refrigerate. Serve at room temperature with extra lemon wedges.

MELENZANE A CAPE E MORTE

Eggplants Tic Tac Toe

6-8 Small eggplant
1 cup of finely chopped peeled tomatoes (Fresh or Canned)
1/4 cup fresh chopped basil
1/4 cup extra virgin olive oil
1 Tablespoon of kosher salt
1 Teaspoon pepper
1 Tablespoon of Parmesan cheese
1 Teaspoon chopped garlic
1/4 teaspoon of dried oregano

Slice eggplant in two, lengthwise. Score the tops like a tic tack toe design. Sprinkle one teaspoon of salt. Add a little water and set aside for half-hour. Meantime prepare mix. Add all the above ingredients in a bowl reserving a little oil for baking pan. Squeeze the salted eggplant removing as much of the water as possible. Fill with mixture into the scored areas. Place in baking dish (glass or ceramic can be used) put a little oil on the bottom. Bake in 350-degree oven for 30 minutes. Lower over at 300 degrees and bake for additional 30 minutes.
Serve as appetizer or side dish

INSALATA DI FAGIOLINI

String Bean Salad

2 lb of green beans
2-tablespoon kosher salt
1/4 cup extra virgin olive oil
2 tablespoon of red wine vinegar
 2 cloves of chopped garlic
2-3 leaves of fresh basil
2-3 quarts of water

Clean and wash beans. Drop in boiling salted water. Cook for about 10 minutes or until tender.
Drain well and transfer to a serving dish. Add oil, vinegar, garlic and basil. Toss well. Add
more salt after tasting if needed.

PARMIGIANA DI MELENZANE

Eggplant Parmesan like My Grandma Used to Make

4 small eggplants or 2 medium ones
2 tablespoon of kosher salt
1 cup of flour
3 eggs
1/2 cup of Parmesan cheese
½ cup of shredded mozzarella cheese (optional)
1-teaspoon black pepper
1-2 cups of vegetable oil
Tomato sauce (recipe in the book)
2-3 leaves of fresh basil (optional)

Peel eggplants (optional) Slice length way about 1/8 of an inch not too thick.
Place in a large dish, salt as you cut layers add a couple of tablespoon of water, repeat until all
the eggplants are cut. Set aside for about 1/2 hour.

Prepare egg mixture.

In a large mixing bowl with fork lightly beat eggs, add pepper, salt and one tablespoon of Parmesan cheese.

Place flour in another dish to coat eggplant.

After1/2 hour, or so squeeze all the water out of eggplants, coat with flour, dip in egg mixture and fry in a large nonstick pan with one cup of the vegetable oil on medium heat, turn once and cook until medium golden brown. Place cooked eggplants on paper towel to drain excess oil. Repeat until done. If necessary add or change oil. Always have about 1 inch of oil in the pan.

    To assemble use tomato sauce (in the book). Have the tomato sauce simmering on stove. In a baking dish, ladle some prepared tomato sauce, then add the cooked eggplants. Alternate with eggplant, tomato sauce and Parmesan cheese, and or mozzarella cheese. Finish last layer with sauce and plenty of Parmesan cheese. Bake for 15 minutes at 350 degrees.

PISELLI E FUNGHI

Peas with Mushrooms

1 Lb. of button mushrooms (clean with towel do not wash)
1 lb. bag of frozen petite peas
1-tablespoon kosher salt
1 large onion (sliced thin)
1/2 teaspoon black pepper
1-tablespoon fresh thyme
1/4 cup extra virgin olive oil
2 cloves garlic finely minced

In a large non-stick pan place oil, garlic and onion; sauté until translucent. Add mushrooms and continue for 5 more minutes on medium. Now add rinsed peas, salt and pepper. Continue to sauté until tender. The cooking time is about 30 minutes total. Add fresh thyme and transfer to a covered casserole dish. Serve warm or at room temperature. Serve as a side dish.

CARCIOFI DI NONNA TERESA

Nonna Teresa's Artichokes

6 Medium Artichokes
1-teaspoon kosher salt
1-teaspoon black pepper
1/4 cup chopped Italian parsley
3 garlic cloves finely chopped
1 cup of water
1/4 cup extra virgin olive oil
1 lemon cut and squeezed

Remove 4-6 outer leaves of the artichokes; Cut the tops and remove stems. Hit the tops of the artichokes on counter to open. Place in cold water with lemon juice and pieces. In a separate bowl, peel the stems and chop, add parsley to stems, add garlic, pepper, 1/2 teaspoon of salt and all the oil but 1 tablespoon (reserve for later use) set aside.

Remove artichokes from water, shake off excess water. With a spoon fill the cavity of each artichoke with stem parsley garlic mixture.

Place in a pot upright; add water and 1/2 teaspoon of salt and 1 tablespoon of oil. Simmer with lid on until tender. Simmer on low heat, test for doneness by removing one outer leaf, (if it comes out easy and it is tender when you taste it, it is ready) serve with a little of the liquid over the artichokes.

FUNGHI IMBOTTITI

Stuffed Mushrooms

20 medium to large button mushrooms
2 slices of white bread, remove crust and put in food processor (make bread crumbs)
1/4 cup grated Parmesan cheese
Salt and pepper to taste

1/2 teaspoon of fresh or dried basil, oregano can be substituted
1/4 cup of extra virgin olive oil
1 chopped garlic clove

Clean mushrooms with a brush or soft cloth, do not wash
Remove stems and roughly chop
Mix all remaining ingredients into the chopped stems, toss lightly
Reserve 1 tablespoon each of olive oil and Parmesan cheese.
Fill mushrooms; place in glass baking dish
Sprinkle reserved Parmesan cheese and oil on top
Bake in 355degree oven for about 30 minutes.

ASPARAGHI CON PANE GRATTUGIATO

Asparagus with Breadcrumbs

2 lbs. Thin asparagus
1/4 cup of extra olive oil
2 chopped garlic cloves
1/4 cup of flavored breadcrumbs
Salt and pepper to taste
2 tablespoon of water
2 tablespoon of grated Parmesan cheese

Wash asparagus; cut approximately 1-2 inches off the stems
Line them in a ceramic or glass ovenproof dish
Add garlic, salt, pepper, cheese, breadcrumbs and olive oil.
Add water on the bottom of dish.
Cover with glass lid or plastic wrap.
Microwave on high for 7 minutes. Let rest for 10 minutes or longer before serving.

PISELLI, PROSCIUTTO E CIPOLLE

Peas with Prosciutto and Onions

16. Oz of frozen peas
1/4 lb of prosciutto (cut in bite size pieces)
1 medium onion (sliced thin)
1/4 cup of extra virgin olive oil
Salt and pepper to taste
1 tsp chopped garlic
1-teaspoon fresh thyme

In medium skillet place oil, garlic and onions, cook until translucent in color add prosciutto. Continue to cook for 2-4 more minutes. Add peas, some black pepper and salt. Continue to cook on medium heat for approximately 15 minutes or until tender. Add fresh thyme. Transfer to a covered dish to keep warm.

SCAROLE STUFATE

Escarole with Capers, Olives and Anchovies

3 escarole
2 tablespoon of olives di Gaeta (remove pits and chop into small pieces)
1 tablespoon capers (use those preserved in vinegar)
3-4 fillets of anchovies
1/4 cup of extra virgin olive oil
1/4 teaspoon of red pepper flakes
1 tsp kosher salt
1 teaspoon of chopped garlic

Discard the first couple of outer leaves of the escarole
Wash escarole well by placing in water in a large bowl. Repeat until all the dirt or sand is gone. Allow to drain for a few minutes.
In heavy skillet heat oil, garlic, olives, capers and anchovies cook for 1-2 minutes. Add escarole and cover quickly. It will sizzle, be careful not to get burned. Add salt and pepper

flakes. Cook with lid on low heat for 15-20 minutes. Taste, add more salt if needed. Transfer to platter and serve with Italian bread with your favorite meat dish or fish.

INSALATA DI FAGIOLINI

String Bean Salad

1 cup of cooked white beans
1 teaspoon of dried oregano
1 clove chopped garlic
1/4 cup extra virgin olive oil
1 small red onion (sliced thin)
1 teaspoon of kosher salt
1/2 cup of Gaeta olives
1 cup of marinated pickled peppers (recipe below)

Place beans in a bowl, add oil, salt, garlic, onion, oregano, olives add peppers and toss.
Serve as a salad or for a light lunch

PEPERONI SOTTO ACETO

Pickled Peppers

20 red round vine ripened red peppers (can be picked at a local farm in late August)
2 Quarts of red wine vinegar
1 Quart of cold water
3 tablespoon of kosher salt
2-3 cloves of garlic peeled left whole
3-4 mason jars quart size, cleaned sterilized

In a clean sterilized glass jar place cleaned peppers (wipe with cloth to clean do not wash them, snip the stems with scissors.
In a large pot, place vinegar, water and salt bring to boil. Turn off the heat and allow cooling.

Pour cooled vinegar mixture in prepared jar with peppers, add garlic and cover. More than one jar maybe needed. Store sealed jars in a cool place for one month before eating.

After one month or longer, remove peppers from vinegar. Cut pepper in half, remove seeds and cut in strips. Now add 1 teaspoon dried oregano, and your favorite olive oil. Place in a plastic container and refrigerate. The peppers can be kept in the refrigerator for a long time. Use them in your favorite antipasto or as a side dish.

MELENZANE SOTTO OLIO

Pickled Eggplant

6 medium eggplants
1/2 cup of kosher salt
2 cloves of chopped garlic
1 dried hot pepper or 1/4 teaspoon of red pepper flakes
1 cup each of extra virgin olive oil and cup of vegetable oil (mix together)
1 cup white vinegar, plus 2 tablespoon
1-cup water
1 teaspoon of dried oregano

Peel the eggplants and slice in two inch long and 1/8 inch thin strips. Place in a large bowl; add 1 cup white vinegar, 1 cup salt and water. Place a plate over and something heavy to press the cut eggplant and to weight it down. Let this sit for at least 3 hours. Later squeeze out the excess liquid from eggplants by fistfuls. Discard vinegar brine.

Repeat until all is done. In a clean bowl place eggplants, one cup of the mixed oil, oregano and pepper flakes, mix and taste. At this time, add the reserved vinegar, oregano and more salt (if needed). Transfer the eggplants into sterilized glass jars, pressing down as you fill top with additional mixed oil, place lids and store in refrigerator for one month before eating and up to a year. Eat with antipasto.

POLPETTINE DI PESCE

Crab cake

1 lb. lump crabmeat
1 egg beaten lightly
1-tablespoon fresh basil
½ teaspoon fresh thyme
2 slices white bread, crust removed (make fresh breadcrumbs in food processor)
1-teaspoon kosher salt
1 /2 teaspoon black pepper
1 clove chopped garlic
1 small onion (chopped)
¼ cup olive oil
1-tablespoon plain yogurt
1 lemon cut in eight

Place one-tablespoon olive oil, chopped onion, and garlic in a skillet. Cook until translucent. Set aside. In a mixing bowl, place breadcrumbs, salt, pepper, and egg. Add crabmeat and yogurt. Add onion mixture. Mix lightly. Divide in eight equal parts. Form into balls and slightly flatten. Refrigerate for 20 minutes. Place the rest of the olive oil in a non-stick large skillet on medium heat. Heat oil; place four crab cakes in skillet. Let one side cook well before turning. It will fall apart. Flip with spatula after about 6 minutes. Cook on the other side until browned nicely. Place on paper towel to drain and repeat.

Serve with a wedge of lemon.

STUFFING

(for turkey or roasting chicken)

1 lb button mushrooms chopped bite size
3 stalks celery chopped bite size
1 large onion chopped bite size
3 cloves chopped garlic
Kosher salt

Pepper
¼ cup olive oil
1-quart vegetable or chicken stock
6 large eggs
¼ cup Parmesan cheese
1-tablespoon fresh sage chopped
1-teaspoon fresh thyme
1 package bread stuffing (any type)

In a large skillet, place oil, mushrooms, celery, onion and garlic. Sauté on medium heat until lightly brown and translucent. Now add salt, pepper and fresh herbs. Stir and set aside to cool. This can be made the day before and placed in the refrigerator.

In a large bowl, place bread and stock. Lightly beat eggs and add to bread. Now add grated cheese and stir in the cooled vegetables. Lightly toss. This stuffing can be cooked in a greased ovenproof dish in the oven at 350 degree or 20 minutes or until lightly browned. This stuffing can also be used to fill the turkey. If stuffing a bird makes sure you close the cavity well. We want to keep all the stuffing in the bird.

ZUCCHINI IMBOTTITI

Stuffed Zucchini

4 medium firm zucchini
2 slices white bread (remove crust) place in food processor and make breadcrumbs
1-teaspoon kosher salt
3-4 fresh basil leaves chopped
1 garlic clove chopped
2-tablespoon olive oil
1 egg
2-tablespoon Parmesan cheese
½ cup shredded mozzarella

Wash zucchini. Slice in half created two open pieces. With melon scooper remove inner part of zucchini. Now coarsely chop the flesh of zucchini, add breadcrumbs, salt, pepper, Parmesan cheese and half of the mozzarella. Stir and add lightly beaten egg and one spoon of olive oil. With a spoon fill the zucchini shells and top with shredded mozzarella. Place one spoon of olive oil on the bottom of the baking dish.

Bake for 25-30 Minutes
Oven at 350 degrees

LENTICCHIE

Lentils

1 cup dry lentils (washed)
2 cups water
1 small onion chopped
1 carrot small cubed
1 celery stalk chopped
½ cup tomatoes, peeled and cut
2-tablespoon olive oil
1 clove chopped garlic
¼ teaspoon each dried basil and oregano
½ teaspoon black pepper (optional)
Kosher salt to taste

In a medium heavy saucepan, place oil, onion, carrots, and celery. Sauté until lightly brown, now add tomatoes and garlic. Add salt, oregano and basil. Cook for a couple of minutes. Now add the dry lentils and water. Allow it to boil, then lower the heat. Cook on medium low for about 25-30 minutes. Taste for the lentils. They should be soft but not mushy. More water can be added if necessary. It should not be soupy. Serve over rice or as a side dish. Drizzle extra virgin olive oil before serving. Hot pepper (optional)

MEAT
AND
FISH

2

POLLO AL FORNO CON PATATE

Roasted Chicken and Potatoes

One medium chicken washed, dried and cut up
8 –10 medium potatoes peeled and sliced ¼ inch thick
1 large sliced onion
Salt and pepper to taste
¼ cup Parmesan cheese
¼ cup extra virgin olive oil
One teaspoon dried oregano
2 cloves chopped garlic
¼ cup white wine

Line roasting pan with chicken
Place potatoes on top add the rest of the ingredients.
Bake in 350 oven for 1 ½ hour turning once
Chicken breasts with rib meat can be substituted.

POLLO CON LIMONE

Chicken with Lemon

One lb. thin chicken cutlets washed and patted dried
¼ cup olive oil
Fresh parsley 3-4 sprigs
Salt 1 teaspoon
Juice one lemon
¼ cup white wine
2 cloves chopped garlic
¼ cup flour
Dredge chicken in flour

Heat a heavy skillet. Add garlic and slightly cook. Add cutlets 3-4 at the time cook on both sides. Add salt on both sides. Cook for 2-3 minutes, turning once. Remove and set aside. Continue until all cooked. Return back to skillet. Add lemon, wine. Reduce sauce and taste Add parsley and serve

POLLO CON CIPOLLE E VINO

Chicken with Onions and Wine

One medium chicken cut, washed and padded dry (Chicken breast with ribs may be used)
2 onions sliced
2 cloves chopped garlic
¼ cup olive oil
Salt 1-2 teaspoon
1/2 cup dry white wine.
 1/2 teaspoon f dried oregano and 2-3 leaves fresh basil (can be left out)

In a large skillet add oil, onions and garlic, cook until translucent. Add chicken and lightly brown on both sides, pour in wine and deglaze. Add salt, oregano, basil and pepper. Cover and cook on low heat for approximately 45 minutes or until chicken is done. Turn several times. Transfer to a serving platter and serve.

VITELLO RIPIENO

Fennel Stuffed Veal

4 lb. boneless butterfly shoulder veal
1/4 lb sliced prosciutto
3 small fennels (washed and sliced thin)
1/2 cup peeled and diced carrot
1 bay leaf
3/4 cup white wine.
6-tablespoon extra virgin olive oil
1 small onion (finely chopped)
1-cup chicken or any homemade broth
Kosher salt and pepper to taste
1-tablespoon fresh parsley
1 medium ripened tomato (chopped)

In a skillet place 2 tablespoon of oil, sliced fennels and 1/2 of the onion. Add salt and pepper to taste. Cook until slightly tender. Place in a dish and set aside.

Dry and place veal on a flat surface to stuff. Place the prosciutto and cooked fennel spreading evenly on the veal. Roll into a log and tie with cooking string in several places to keep the stuffing from coming out.

In a separate broiling pan. Place the remaining oil, onion, carrots, and tomato and the rolled veal. Brown on stove for a few minutes on both sides. Deglaze with 1/4 cup of wine. Add the bay leaf and the rest of the wine, salt and pepper. Transfer the pan to a 350-degree oven and roast for an additional hour and 10 minutes. Remove from oven and let it rest for 10 minutes. Slice and add the cooked chopped vegetable over the slices. Sprinkle the fresh parsley and Serve.

SPICOLA

Red Snapper

2 lbs. Red snapper fillet
1 cup chopped and peeled tomatoes
1 tablespoon drained capes
1 teaspoon chopped garlic
1/4 teaspoon red pepper flakes
1/4 cup extra virgin olive oil
1/4 cup pitted gaeta or cured olives
1/4 teaspoon dried oregano

In a large skillet heat oil, garlic and tomatoes. Cook for 10 minutes medium heat. Add fish, capers, hot pepper, olives and oregano. Cover and cook on low to medium heat for additional 15 minutes. Transfer to a serving platter; pour the tomato sauce on top, before serving.

CALAMARI FRITTI

Fried Calamari (Cathryns Favorite)

2 pound cleaned cut calamari
Juice one lemon and 1 cut up in wedges for garnish
1-cup flour
2 cups vegetable oil
Salt and pepper

Pat dries the cleaned calamari and dredge into flour. Heat the vegetable oil in a large non-stick pan. Drop some of the calamari coated with flour (shake off excess flour) Cook until golden. Repeat until all are cooked. Place cooked calamari on a paper towel to absorb excess oil. Transfer to a serving platter. Add salt pepper and a squeeze of lemon. Serve with extra lemon wedges.

BACCALA

Cod Fish

This fish is purchased dried and salted. It is prepared mostly at Christmas time or during the winter season. Before it can be prepared, it must be soaked in cold water for three to four days. You also need to change the water once a day until the fish is ready to be cooked. It can be purchased in most specialty markets. It is sold with bones and without. For these recipes we prefer the one without the bones. Once you buy the dried codfish it should be cut in four to five inch rectangles before soaking. Place it in a large bowl, add cold water to cover. Cover with a lid or wrap. Place it in a cool place. It does not need to be refrigerated. After 3-4 days of soaking with water changes once daily, it can be placed in freezer bags and stored in the freezer, up to a month. It can be refrigerated in a sealed container up to three days before cooking. Here are a few of my dad's favorite ways to prepare bacccala

INSALATA DI BACCALA

Cod Salad

4-6 thicker pieces soaked codfish
1/4 cup extra virgin olive oil
2 cloves chopped garlic
1/2 cup fresh parsley
1/2 cup Gaeta olive or dried cured black olives
1 cup pickled red peppers (recipe in the book) optional
4-5 quarts water

In a large pot bring cold water to a boil, add the codfish and cook on high for about 15 minutes or until it starts to flake. Carefully remove with slotted spoon from water and place on a serving platter. Allow to cool. When it has cooled remove skin and break apart into smaller pieces. Add the oil, garlic, parsley, lemon juice, olive and peppers. Toss lightly and taste. Salt can be added if necessary.

FRIED BACCALA

Fried Cod

4-6 thinner pieces of soaked codfish
1 cup or more vegetable oil
1-cup flour
Salt and pepper

Place the soaked codfish on paper towels to remove excess moisture. In a plate place flour and pepper. Lightly four the codfish and set aside. In a nonstick deep frying pan, add 1 cup of vegetable oil or about 2 inches, allow to heat. Place codfish carefully in the hot oil and cook on each side for about 10 minutes until golden and crispy. Remove and place of clean paper towel to absorb excess oil. Extra pepper and salt can now be added. Serve hot.

ZUPPA DI BACCALA

Codfish Stew

4-6 large all purpose potatoes
4-5 pieces codfish
1 small onion (sliced thin)
1-cup tomato sauce
1/2 cup chopped and peeled ripened tomatoes
1-2 teaspoon kosher salt
1/4 cup extra virgin olive oil
1 teaspoon dried oregano
1/4 teaspoon red pepper flakes
1/2 cup cold water.

Peel and cut potatoes into one-inch cubes. Place in cold water. In a large saucepan, place oil, add sliced onion and lightly brown. Remove the sliced potatoes from water and add to pot. Add one teaspoon of salt. Tomato sauce, chopped tomatoes, oregano and red pepper flakes. Also add the cold water. Place heat on low to medium and cook for about 20 minutes or when the potatoes are slightly tender. Now add codfish. Place on top of potatoes and cover. Cook an additional 10 minutes. Turn the heat off and allow to rest. Serve with crusty Italian bread.

INVOLITINI DI POLLO

Chicken Rolletini

8 slices of thin chicken cutlets (veal can be substituted)
1/4 lb. prosciutto sliced thin
1/4 lb. Provolone sliced thin
2 tablespoon chopped parsley
1/4 cup white wine
Salt and pepper to taste
1 clove garlic finely chopped
1/4 cup extra virgin olive oil
¼ cup chicken or vegetable stock
1 small package mushrooms cleaned and sliced (optional)

Place one piece of chicken on a clean plate, place 1 piece of cheese, 1 piece of prosciutto, a little parsley and pepper roll up and close with a wooden tooth pick. Repeat until all cutlets have been rolled. In a large skillet heat olive oil with garlic and mushrooms, sauté for 5-7 minutes add chicken and sauté on high heat turning once to brown both sides. Add salt and pepper to taste. Now add wine to deglaze. Pour in stock. And lower heat.
Cook on low to medium heat with lid on. Additional 10-15 minutes of cooking.
Makes 4-6 servings.

POLLO ALLA GRIGLIA

Grilled chicken

6 chicken breasts or 1 whole chicken cut up
1-tablespoon kosher salt
2-tablespoon extra virgin olive oil
1/4 cup each fresh mint, parsley, basil
1-tablespoon fresh rosemary
1-tablespoon fresh thyme
Juice of one lemon
4-cloves garlic chopped

Clean chicken, place in a shallow baking dish add all the above ingredients and allow to marinate overnight or at least 3 hours. Place on hot grill and cook until done. Brush with remainder of herb mixture for the first 10 minutes of cooking. The breasts will cook in 15-20 on medium heat. The cut up chicken will take approximately 1 hour on low to medium heat. Serve with vinaigrette (recipe to follow)

SALMONE ALLA GRIGLIA

Grilled Salmon

2 lb. Skinned and filet salmon
2-tablespoon extra virgin olive oil
1 tsp mustard
1-tablespoon soy sauce
1-teaspoon kosher salt
1-tablespoon fresh chopped parsley
1 lemon sliced in boats for garnish
2 gloves chopped garlic

Cut salmon in 4 equal portions, clean and place in a shallow baking dish. Add all the above ingredients except lemon. Refrigerate and marinate for 3 hours. Grill on medium heat turning once. Serve with lemon wedges and a drizzle of olive oil. Serves 4 people

SALSA DI ERBETTE E ACETO

Herb Vinaigrette for Garnish

1 clove of finely chopped garlic
1 tablespoon each of thyme, mint, basil and parsley (fresh is preferred)
Salt and pepper to taste
1 juiced lemon and one cut in wedges for garnish
1 tablespoon of balsamic vinegar
2 tablespoon of extra virgin olive oil

———

Mix together and drizzle over your favorite grilled fish or chicken
This can be refrigerated for later use

SALSICCE CON PATATE E PEPPERONI

Roast Italian sausage with potatoes and onion

1 lb. Italian sausage
Salt and pepper to taste
1 tablespoon grated Parmesan cheese
1/4 tsp dried oregano
1/4 tsp garlic powder or 1 teaspoon of chopped garlic
6-8 medium potatoes peel and slice 1/4 inch thick
1 medium onion sliced thin
1/4 cup extra virgin olive oil

———

Place sausages in a large roasting pan, place l sliced potatoes and onion over the sausage, add oil and spices. Place in 375-degree oven for 1 1/2 hour.
Turn half way thru cooking time
Serves 4-6 people

BRASATO CON PENNE

Veal Florentine with Penne (Vincent's Favorite)

4 veal chops or 1 large veal steak
1 medium onion
2 stalks celery
2 small carrots or 8 mini carrots
6-8 springs fresh parsley
Salt and pepper to taste
1 cup white wine
1/4 cup extra virgin olive oil
2 tablespoons flour
1 chopped garlic clove
2-3 tablespoon Parmesan cheese
1/2 cup stock or water

In a food processor, or a mini chopper, chop onion, celery, carrots, garlic and parsley.
In a large heavy skillet, place oil, and chopped vegetable, salt and pepper. Sauté until vegetable have softened. Move the vegetable on the side and add veal. Season with salt and pepper. Brown both side.
 On medium to high heat. Pour wine to deglaze. Now lower heat and with lid on, cook for 1 ½ to 2 hours. Stir occasionally. If liquids reduce too much add 1/4 cup of water continue cooking until meat is tender. In separate bowl mix flour with cold stock or water, making slurry. Add to the cooked meat, bring to a simmer and cook for a couple more minutes to cook out the flour. .

Meanwhile cook penne al dente in salted water. Strain the penne; add to veal sauce, add Parmesan cheese and serve. The veal can be served with a salad or with pasta.
Serves 4-6 people.

COTOLETTE DI POLLO

Chicken Cutlets

6-8 thinly sliced chicken breast
1 cup flavored breadcrumbs
2 eggs
1-tablespoon Parmesan cheese
Salt and pepper to taste
Vegetable oil for frying

———

Wash the cutlets pat dry with paper towel
In a bowl beat eggs, cheese, salt and pepper
Dip in egg wash and then into the bread crumbs coating on both sides
In a nonstick skillet add oil on medium heat place chicken cutlets; turn once until golden brown
Place on paper towel to drain oil, serve immediately with lemon wedge (optional)

POLPETTE

Nonna Caterina's Meatballs

1 lb. Chopped pork meat
1/2 lb chopped veal
1/2 lb chopped beef
Two slices day old Italian bread (peasant type preferred)
3 eggs lightly beaten
2 tablespoon grated Parmesan cheese
1-teaspoon kosher salt and 1/2 teaspoon of black pepper
1-tablespoon fresh chopped parsley.
1/2 cup olive oil for frying.

———

Soak bread in water, squeeze excess water and add to meat. Add eggs and the rest of the ingredients, the mixture should be soft even a little runny. Heat olive oil in a skillet heat on medium heat. Shape meatball by wetting your hands forming into golf size balls. Place in skillet and cook turning until dark golden brown. Can be eaten fried or placed in red tomato sauce. If you a using them in sauce, the meatball should be slightly undercooked. They will continue to cook in the tomato sauce.

CHICKEN CACCIATORE

Hunter style chicken

1 chicken (cleaned, skinned and cut up)
1 large onion
1 teaspoon chopped garlic
1/4 cup white wine
1-teaspoon oregano dried
1/2 cup peeled chopped tomatoes
Kosher salt approximately 1 tablespoon
1/4 cup of extra virgin olive oil

———————

In large skillet place oil, onion and garlic cook until translucent add cut up chicken and cook on medium to high heat turning once to lightly brown, add wine, oregano salt and cook with cover on.

Lower heat and continue cooking for about 45 minutes. Forming a well in the center of the skillet place chopped tomatoes cook for 5 minutes and stir into chicken. Let cook for 5 more minutes on low and with the lid on. To serve remove the chicken and place on a platter add some of the sauce. Pour the rest into a small bowl to allow for individual serving over chicken. Serves 4-6 people

CAPONE IMBOTTITO AL FORNO

Capon Stuffed and roasted

4-5 lb. capon or roasting chicken
2-tablespoon kosher salt
1/4 cup white vinegar
2 cloves minced garlic
1/4 teaspoon dried oregano
2-tablespoon Parmesan cheese
1-teaspoon black pepper
1/4 cup extra virgin olive oil
1 stuffing recipe (see book)
1 large onion sliced

1/4 cup dried white wine

Two to three hours before roasting and stuffing the capon. Clean capon, and place in a large bowl with 2 tablespoon kosher salt and vinegar and allow sitting for a couple of hours. Later remove from water and pat dry. Spoon in the prepared stuffing into the cavity of the capon. Now with needle and white thread sew closed the cavity. (Keeping stuffing in the capon)
In a large roasting pan place the stuffed capon, and then sprinkle on the pepper, dried oregano, black pepper, garlic and olive oil. Place sliced onion around the pan, add wine. Place in a 375-degree preheated oven. During the cooking process. Pour some of the juices over top. Cook 20 minutes per pound or until juices run clear. Remove from oven and allow resting for 15 minutes before carving. Remove the string and slide stuffing out and slice. Slice capon and pour pan juices over before serving.

IMBETTONO

Stuffing

2 Lb. Button mushrooms chopped
1 package cubed dried stuffing mix
1/4 cup extra virgin olive oil
3 stalks celery chopped
1 large onion chopped
Kosher salt
2 cloves minced garlic
1-teaspoon black pepper
1/4 cup Parmesan cheese
1-tablespoon fresh thyme
1-tablespoon fresh Italian parsley
4 eggs
1-quart chicken stock or vegetable stock

Clean and cut mushrooms in small bite size pieces. Dice onion and celery. Place 3 tablespoon of olive oil in a non-stick pan; add mushrooms, onion, celery, and garlic salt to taste and pepper. Cook until tender and set aside.

In a large bowl lightly beat eggs, add salt, pepper and cheese. Add cubed bread, broth, thyme and cooked mushroom mixture and toss lightly. Add 2 tablespoon of olive oil. Transfer to an oiled baking dish and bake for 1 hour at 350 degrees. Stuff your turkey or any roasting chicken

PASTAS, SAUCES AND SOUPS

3

PASTA

Served at our house seven days a week when we were growing up. Special pasta would be served on Sundays and holidays, my mother would made homemade egg noodles or tagliatelle all'uovo. The art of cooking good pasta whether dried or fresh pasta is simple. Always start with a large pot of water. Fill the pot three quarters of the way up with cold water, cover and bring to a boil. Salt the water before putting in the pasta. One handful of salt per pound of pasta is generally sufficient. Always stir the pasta as you boil it. Cook dried pasta or pasta in a box purchased at the supermarket until tender and firm or as we say al dente. Fresh pasta or homemade pasta cooks a little quicker. Follow these simple steps and your results will always be good.

CANNING SAUCE

Ever since I can remember. My family has been canning tomato sauce for the entire year. Every August during the tomato season we have been processing hundreds of mason jars filled with tomato sauce for the yearly consumption. It is done one day in the backyard with now, modern tools, but years ago with hand machines. We buy bushels of tomatoes from a woman who gets them from a local farm delivered to her house. Hundreds of bushels ordered by several families in the community get delivered.

Everyone waits for the phone call from this person to say it is time to pick up the tomatoes, they have arrived. Some people grow or pick their own tomatoes at a local farm or their backyard also. The process is pretty simple. It can also be done in your kitchen on a much smaller scale. We reuse mason jar for the process. At a local hardware store we purchase new lids every year. The mason jars get washed in the dishwasher as we empty them and before storing away for the next harvest.

A large propane burner is used to place a huge cooking pot on it. The tomatoes are washed and placed in boiling water. We cook them until the skin brakes or crack. Then we process the cooked tomatoes by using electric sauce machines, which separates the sauce and the skin. The sauce is then lightly salted and placed in the clean jar with a few leaves of fresh basil. We then seal them. When all the jars are filled and sealed they are then placed in a large steel drum or large pot over the propane burner. The jars are laid down. Some old towels or blankets cushion the bottom of the drum. Water is then added to the pot. The pot is covered and the heat is turned on. It takes one to two hours for the water to come to a simmering boil. From the time it starts to boil we continue to cook for 1 1/2 hour. Then heat is then turned off. We leave the drum or pot to sit overnight. The next day, the jars are removed from the drum and stored in the basement in a dry cool place. These jars can be stored for months or until the next process. They will stay on the shelf for years if done correctly.

This can be attempted on a much smaller scale in your kitchen. Follow the same method.

We also do the same technique with sliced ripened tomatoes. These tomatoes can be considered stewed tomatoes. We use these tomatoes for adding to soups and stews. They are also great for spaghetti sauce and pizza sauce. Here how it goes.

Wash the tomatoes and remove any dark spots. It works best on plum tomatoes and real ripened ones. After washing cut tomato in half and shake of some seeds. In a large bowl add some salt. Then fill the same clean mason jars, any size will do. Make sure to push down the tomato pieces so the jars are filled well; add 2-3 leaves of fresh basil and seal. Follow the same process in the water as the tomato sauce. When you use these tomatoes, the skin is easily removed; they can be chopped or left whole. When you use the jars whether it is the sauce or tomato pieces, you need to cook them before adding to your favorite pasta or stews.

SUNDAY SAUCE

2 quarts tomato sauce
1/4 cup extra virgin olive oil
1/2 small onion sliced thin
1-2 cloves garlic left whole (remove it after browning)
1 lb. Thin sliced meat for rolling (flank steak or any sliced beef works well)
1/4 cup fresh parsley
1/4 teaspoon fresh black pepper
1 clove garlic chopped (additional for meat)
String for tying meat
1-tablespoon kosher salt
1/4 cup red wine
4-5 leaves fresh basil (dried can be substituted)

Place meat down on a plate and put a little each of pepper, parsley, garlic and salt, chopped garlic is optional. Roll like a jellyroll and secure with string in several places. Set aside. In large saucepan place oil, garlic and chopped onion and a little salt, cook until lightly brown add prepared rolled meat and sauté. Brown on all sides add 1/4 cup of red wine and cook for about five more minutes. Add tomato sauce, basil and salt. Cover and continue cooking on medium low for an additional hour. Stir several times while cooking. Prepared meatballs can also be added to the saucepot. Add the meatballs 15 minutes before the sauce is done cooking. (meatball recipe in the book)

This sauce or ragu would be made every Sunday or on every holiday. Pasta dried or fresh would be then cooked and added with lots of cheese on top. After church on Sunday we would walk in to the smell of this wonderful sauce. My mother would then give us a piece of homemade bread with a large spoonful of the cooking sauce on it. These are the memories that still linger in my mind today when I make sauce.
Just the other day my son tried bread with a spoonful of sauce on it and said, ma, this is good and then I proceeded to tell him the story about Sundays after church.
I have been helping my mother cook ever since I can remember. She has never used a measuring cup for any of these great recipes. I too, cook in this manner. Cooking comes within and it is a passion that drives you to prepare such wonderful meals. It's the smell and the joy of preparing food that please your eyes and those whom you love. Don't worry so much about the measuring cups and spoons just have fun and most important use fresh and natural ingredients like our mothers and grandmothers used from our motherland.

BASILICO SECCO

Dried Basil

2 cups or more basil leaves
1 large cookie sheet
1 large piece wax paper

———

Wash and dry basil leaves well. Place on wax paper on cookie sheet and place in a 200-degree oven for 2 hours. Turn off the oven and leave overnight. The next day. Crumble the dry basil with your hands. Place in a strainer and press thru. The basil will be fine and beautiful. Place in a jar with lid on. Use smaller amounts if using dried in your recipe. It is concentrated when dried. I prefer dried when fresh is not available and rather than using basil that has been froze.

SUGO SEMPLICE DI POMODORO

Basic Italian Tomato Sauce

2 Quarts canned tomato sauce (recipe for canning is in the book) or store bought
1 chopped garlic clove
1/4 onion sliced thin
1 tablespoon kosher or sea salt
1/4 cup extra virgin olive oil
4-5 fresh basil leaves

———

In a medium saucepan heat oil, garlic and onion, cook until light brown.
Add tomato sauce, salt and basil
Cook on low heat for 20-30 minutes.
This sauce can be used on eggplant parmesan, on pasta and many other things.
It is a basic sauce without meat.

PESTO

2 cups washed and dried fresh basil leaves

2 cloves peeled garlic
1-teaspoon kosher salt
½ cup extra virgin olive oil
1/4 cup parmiggiano reggiano (used later when pasta is mixed with prepared pesto)
1/4 cup walnuts (optional) or ¼ cup pignoli nuts

In food process combine all ingredients, Blend well until smooth.
Use immediately over cooked pasta, or store in plastic container topping it with some olive oil.
It will also freeze well. I freeze the pesto in silicone ice cube trays. Once frozen remove and place in a freezer bag or container. Store in freezer for several months. Defrost or just simple place under hot cooked pasta. Add a little extra virgin olive oil and a little pasta water. Toss and top with cheese.

Cook one pound of your favorite pasta (fusilli work well)

Drain when pasta is al dente
Mix cold pesto sauce with Parmesan cheese, toss and serve
Serves 6-8 people

SCAROLE E FAGIOLI

Escarole and Beans

1-2 heads escarole
4 cups boiling water
1-cup navy or cannellini beans cooked.
2-tablespoon kosher salt

Wash cut and drains escarole. Boil water add one tablespoon of salt, drop in cleaned escarole.
Cook until tender approximately 15 minutes. Drain and set aside. Discard water
In a heavy saucepan lightly brown two chopped cloves of garlic with ¼ cup of olive oil
Add cooked escarole slightly chopped
Add one cup of cooked white beans

Add 1 cup of water
Salt to taste
Allow to simmer on medium heat for 15 minutes
Serve with Italian bread or corn pizza (recipe in the book)

BRODO DI POLLO

Nonna Teresa's Chicken soup

4 quarts water
½ cleaned cup up chicken
2 peeled medium potatoes
2 large peeled and cut carrots
1 medium onion peeled not cut
3-4 tomatoes well ripened tomatoes (use homemade canned one you have)
One large celery stalk with leaves cut up
2-tablespoon kosher salt
1 bunch fresh parsley
2-3 leaves basil if available

Four quarts of cold water, bring to boil, add chicken and salt, skim the foam well and reduce heat to low. This will give you nice clear broth. Skim the foam well, to achieve nice clear broth. Now add all the herbs and vegetables. Simmer on medium heat, cover with lid leaving a little space. Cook the chicken soup for about 2 hours.
In a separate pot follow boiling pasta instructions. Cook your favorite small pastas or tortellini. Add soup, chicken and vegetables. Serve immediately. Grated parmesan cheese can be added before serving in individual bowls.
Serve cooked soup with Small pasta or tortellini

TORTELLINI IN BRODO

Tortellini with chicken soup

1 lb fresh or frozen tortellini
1-tablespoon kosher salt

Cook tortellini in 4 quarts boiling salted water al dente.
drain well and mix in with nonna Teresa chicken soup.
Soup can be strained if you don't like all the vegetables.
Serve with chicken, vegetables and broth.

PASTA E FAGIOLI

Pasta with beans

1 cup cooked white navy beans or cannellini beans
1 lb tubetti medium size pasta
2 cups tomato sauce and 1/2 cup of crushed peeled tomatoes
2-tablespoon extra virgin olive oil
1-teaspoon kosher salt
4-5 fresh basil leaves
1 clove chopped garlic
Black pepper

In a medium pot place oil and garlic cook for 1 minute. Add tomatoes, tomato sauce, salt and basil. Cook on low heat for 15 minutes. A little water can be added if the sauce gets to dry while cooking.
Meanwhile cook the tubetti pasta in 4 quarts of salted water al dente. Drain pasta leaving a little boiling liquid in it. Add the cooked beans and prepared sauce. Mix well and serve (black pepper can be added to the plate)
My grandpa, Antonio would eat pasta e fagioli with a slice of homemade bread.

ZUPPA DI VEGETALI

Vegetable Stew (ciambotta)

1 small chopped onion
1 stalk chopped celery
2-3 medium peeled and chopped carrots
1-2 medium zucchini (cubed)
4-6 large peeled and cubed potatoes

1/2 cup frozen or fresh peas
1-cup tomato sauce or one cup of peeled chopped tomatoes
2-3 leaves fresh basil
1 teaspoon dried oregano
1-2 teaspoon kosher salt
¼ cup extra virgin olive oil
1/2-cup broth or water

Lightly brown onion, garlic and celery with the olive oil in a medium saucepan.
Add all remaining ingredients except for the zucchini. Simmer on medium to low heat, covering the pot with lid. Cook for about 10 minutes or until potatoes are almost tender. Now add the reserved zucchini and broth or water. Continue cooking for 5 to 10 minutes. Taste and adjust salt. When the potatoes are fork tender the stew is done. Turn heat off and allow to rest before serving. Serve with crusty Italian bread or over rice.

PASTA ALL'UOVO

Fettucine

6 large eggs
3-4 cups unbleached flour
1-tablespoon kosher salt

In a large bowl place cracked eggs, salt, beat lightly. Add flour one cup at a time until a ball forms. Transfer to floured board and continue to knead by hand until smooth. Five to ten minutes should be enough. Cover the large ball and set on the side. Divide the ball in thirds and roll with rolling pin forming a large 15 to 18 inch circle. Dry the sheets by placing on floured surface use an old clean tablecloth to dry rolled circles on your kitchen table. Continue to roll until all done. Let the circles dry for about1/ 2 hours before cutting. When you are ready to cut the fettucine, fold the circle in half and sprinkle some flour, then fold the half circle in half again and re flour. With a sharp serrated knife start slicing the fettuccine about 1/4 in thick and set aside until you have completed the entire process. Flour the cut pasta to prevent sticking even when it is cut. Meanwhile bring a large pot of water to boil, add salt. Drop in cut homemade pasta. Cook for five to ten minutes or until the pasta rises to the top. Drain well, add your favorite sauce and toss lightly. Serve extra sauce in individual bowls topping with Parmesan cheese. Serves 8-10 people

PASTA CON CAULIFIORE

Pasta with Cauliflower

1 head cauliflower (cut into florets)
¼ cup extra virgin olive oil
1 cup peeled and chopped tomatoes
1-cup tomato sauce
2-4 leaves fresh basil
Salt to taste
¼ teaspoon red pepper flakes
1 chopped clove garlic
1 lb of tubetti (ditalini) pasta

Wash and floret the cauliflower, set aside. In a medium saucepan add oil and garlic lightly brown... Add in tomato sauce and chopped tomatoes. Now add salt, pepper flakes and basil. Add in the washed florets of cauliflower. Cook on low heat cover until tender. Cover the pot with lid.
Meanwhile in a large pot of boiling salted water cook the tubetti al dente. Drain the pasta leaving a little wet then adds to the sauce. Stir lightly and serve.

SPAGHETTI CON BROCCOLI DI RAPE

Spaghetti with Broccoli Rabe

1-2 bunches of broccoli rabe
1 Lbs. spaghetti
1/ 4 cup extra virgin olive oil
1-tablespoon kosher salt
1/4 teaspoon red pepper flakes
2 cloves chopped garlic

Clean and remove tough leaves of broccoli rabe wash and drain
In a large skillet place olive oil, garlic and pepper flakes.
Lightly brown garlic, add drained broccoli rabe and salt. Cover immediately and cook on medium heat until tender (this should only take about 10 minutes)

In a large pot of boiling and salted water cook spaghetti al dente.
Drain leaving a little of the liquid water in them.
Immediately add to cooked broccoli rabe and toss.
More pepper flakes can be added at the table

PASTIERA

Pasta Casserole (Served on Holy Saturday)

8 Oz. package long grain rice
12 oz egg noodles or any type of linguini
8 oz tubetti pasta
1/2 cup extra virgin olive oil
2 whole garlic cloves (lightly mash back of knife to release oils)
1/2 cup grated parmesan cheese
Salt and pepper to taste
4 eggs lightly beaten

In a large pot filled ¾ with water. Allow to boil, add salt. Now add rice and allow cooking for 5 minutes. Then add the tubetti and linguini. Cook until it is al dente. Drain leaving about ¼ cup of boiling liquid. While pasta and rice are cooking, in a separate pan add oil and garlic on very low heat just to release garlic flavor and heat oil. Remove garlic and add to the drained pasta rice mixture.

In large pasta bowl beat eggs and cheese. Combine egg mixture and pasta rice mixture together. Grease a glass casserole dish or lasagna pan with olive oil; pour the pasta mixture in it, adding a little oil to the top. Bake for 30 minutes in a preheated 350-degree oven.
Serve hot or room temperature
Can be reheated up to three days
Serves 6-8 people

PASTA E PISELLI

Pasta with Peas

1 lb tubetti pasta
1-teaspoon kosher salt
 8 oz package frozen peas
1 medium onion
2-3 pieces sliced prosciutto
1/4 cup extra virgin olive oil
1/4 cup water

In a medium saucepan lightly sauté finely sliced onion and prosciutto with extra virgin olive oil. Add peas, water and continue to simmer. Cook until peas are tender (about 15 minutes. Meanwhile, cook the dubiety (follow directions on pasta cooking). Drain the pasta leaving a little wet. Add the cooked peas and prosciutto to the drained pasta. Stir and serve immediately. Extra black pepper can be added to individual plates.
Serves 4-6 people

PASTA E PATATE

Pasta and Potatoes

1 lb tubetti or favorite small pasta
3-4 peeled potatoes, peeled and cubed about 1/4 inch
1/2 cup cut celery including leaves
1 small onion
3-4 chopped seeded and peeled ripe tomatoes
1/4 cup extra virgin olive oil
Salt to taste
2-3 leaves fresh basil
1/4 cup water

Sauté onion and celery in a medium saucepan with oil add potatoes, tomatoes, salt basil and water. Cover and simmer on low for about 20 minutes or until potatoes are tender.

Meanwhile bring salted boiling water to boil cook pasta al dente, drain leaving a little wet, add to potato sauce and serve.
Serves 4-6 people

CAMILLO'S FAVORITE SPAGHETTI

with basil and tomato sauce

8-10 ripened plum tomatoes (wash and cut in 4 removing seeds)
2 chopped garlic cloves
1/4 cup extra olive oil
6- 8 fresh leaves of basil
Salt to taste

———

Lightly brown garlic in oil add tomatoes, salt and basil. Cook of medium for bout 15 minutes. Meanwhile cook spaghetti al dente. Drain well and add to tomato sauce, (reserve a little to add to each plate) Serve immediately. Hot pepper flakes can now be added if desired. Serves 4-6 people

ARRABBIATA SAUCE

1-diced onion
1/4 lb. Sliced and diced prosciutto
1/4 cup extra virgin olive oil
1/4 teaspoon red pepper flakes
16 oz can peel chopped tomatoes
2 ounces heavy cream
salt to taste
fresh chopped parsley for garnish

———

In a skillet place oil and onion a little salt and lightly brown. Add in prosciutto and pepper flakes. Cook for a minute add in tomatoes and continue cooking on low heat for an additional 15 minutes. The last 5 minutes add in cream and bring to a simmer. Turn off the heat.
Cook a pound of penne. Add half of the sauce. Serve with additional reserved sauce and extra hot pepper.

SPAGHETTI AGLIO E OLIO

Spaghetti with Garlic and Oil

3 cloves garlic chopped
1/4 cup extra virgin olive oil
3-4 fillets anchovies in olive oil
1/4 teaspoon red pepper flakes
1/4 teaspoon dried oregano
1/4 cup Gaeta olives or cured black olives
1-tablespoon capers rinsed
1-pound spaghetti

In skillet place oil, garlic, let lightly brown on medium heat then add anchovies cook until dissolved add in the pepper flakes, capers, olives and oregano. Cook for 1-2 minutes longer. Add 2-3 tablespoon of pasta water. Simmer for additional 2 minutes. Turn off the heat. Meanwhile in a large pot of water bring to boil. Salt the water and cook spaghetti al dente. Drain and add to previously cooked garlic sauce. Toss lightly and serve

FAGIOLINI E SPAGHETTI

String beans and Spaghetti

2 lbs green beans
1 lb. Spaghetti
1 basic tomato recipe (in the book)
Salt to taste
Lots of water to boil beans and spaghetti (separately)

Clean and wash beans. Place in salted boiling water and cook for 5-10 minutes. Drain and set aside.

Meanwhile prepare basic tomato sauce. When the sauce is almost done place the cooked string beans in the sauce and simmer for 5-10 more minutes on low heat.

In a large pot boil water for spaghetti add salt and cook. Drain well and mix with the tomato and string bean

SUGO

Tomato Sauce for pasta and meatballs

1 clove garlic (chopped)
1 small onion (sliced)
1-quart tomato sauce (recipe for canning tomato sauce in the book)
2-3 leaves fresh basil (dried can be used) recipe in the book
2-tablespoon olive oil
Kosher salt 1 teaspoon

In a medium sauce pan place oil, sliced onion and clove of garlic light brown (onion and garlic can be removed or left in) Add tomato sauce, basil and salt cook for approximately 15-20 minutes on medium-low heat add meatballs previously fried and continue to cook for 20 more minutes.

Sauce can be served on your favorite pasta with meatballs.
Serves 4-6 people

SUGO DI FUNGHI

Porcini with tomato sauce

1 medium sliced onion
2 cloves chopped garlic
1-teaspoon hot pepper flakes
1/4 cup white wine
2-tablespoon extra virgin olive oil
1/2 cup of fresh or dried porcini mushrooms (if dry place in water to soften then chop to add later)
1 teaspoon of dried oregano
1 teaspoon of kosher salt
16 ounces of chopped peeled tomatoes or tomato sauce

In a skillet place oil, onion and garlic, lightly brown then add mushroom let sauté for 5 more minutes, add salt, wine, pepper flakes and oregano sauté for 5 more minutes then add tomato mixture. On low heat cook for 15 minutes. Taste and add more salt if necessary.

Meanwhile in a large pot bring 3 quarts of water to boil and 1 tablespoon of salt and cook 1 lb. of your favorite fettuccine, drain al dente add to sauce, reserve some sauce to place on top as you serve.
Serves 4-6 people

PUTTANESCA SAUCE

Sauce with olives anchovies and capers

2-tablespoon extra virgin olive oil
1-tablespoon capers (in vinegar or salt) rinse to use
20 pitted olives (Italian cured olives or gaeta olives and be used)
2-3 fillet anchovies in oil
16 oz peeled chopped tomatoes
1 tsp dried pepper flakes or hot chili red fresh peppers can be used
1 teaspoon dried oregano
2-3 cloves chopped garlic

In medium skillet heat oil add garlic on low heat lightly brown; add anchovies, olives, capers and pepper flakes cook for 2-5 minutes. Add tomato mixture and oregano taste and add salt if necessary continue to cook on low heat for an additional 15 minutes. Meanwhile in a large pot bring 3-4 quarts of salted water to boil add 1 lb. of spaghetti and cook al dente. Drain and add to sauce, toss and serve
Serves 4-6 people

TACCUNI E FASULI

Beans With Noodles

Perhaps this recipe is the most original from where we come from. A small town called Durazzano, about 30 minutes north of Naples. This dish is the simplest and peasant dish I can think of that my grandmother and mother made. The noodles are made from just flour salt and water. I imagine it was made this way because eggs were not always available or perhaps saved for other meals or baking. Wheat flour was always available, because almost everyone in town would farm wheat in their farms large or small. There was a flourmill in town at least there was one when I was growing up.

RECIPE FOR NOODLES

3-4 cups of unbleached flour
1-tablespoon kosher salt
1/2 cup cold water

———

Make a well with the flour and salt, and then add water a little at a time until a ball forms. Knead the dough for about 5 minutes. Divide the dough in 2 equal balls and roll out on well floured board. Allow the two circles to dry placing them on a clean kitchen cloth with a little flour. About 1-2 hours later cut the noodles. Fold the circle in half then fold in half again. Cut long strips lengthwise three inches in width You can now cut the long strip buy stacking 2 or three on top of each other and cut the short ends. The thickness should resemble that of a noodle or fettuccine. Continue until you have cut them all. Leave on floured towel until you are ready to boil them.

SAUCE FOR NOODLES AND BEANS

A Basic tomato sauce can be followed for this recipe. You can find it in the book.
In addition a 1-cup of cooked cannelloni or white navy beans are needed.

Recipe to cook white beans

1 lb. of dry white navy beans or cannellini
1 tablespoon of kosher salt

———

Wash and soak beans overnight. The cooking process will go faster
Place soaked beans in a large pot. Cover with cold water, 2 cloves of whole garlic and 3 pieces of celery. Bring to boil and lower heat. Cook until tender. You may need to add more water. Salt the beans just about 5 minutes before the cooking process is done. Allow to completely cool. Unused beans can be stored in a container in the refrigerator for up to three day. Small containers can be placed in the freezer for later use.

To complete this dish, here is what we do.

Bring a large pot of water to boil. Salt well and drop in noodles. Boil for about 5 minutes. Drain but leave a little wet, add in tomato sauce and beans, stir gently and allow to heat thru. Serve immediately with fresh black pepper or red pepper flakes.

TAGLIOLINI IN BRODO

Thin noodles with broth

3 large eggs
3-4 cups unbleached flour
1-teaspoon salt

In a food processor place eggs and one cup of flour plus the teaspoon of salt and mix. Add more flour until a ball forms. Remove from processor and knead on a floured board for 3 or 4 minutes. Divide the dough into 6 equal parts. With a pasta machine stretch dough and form thin sheets of pasta. Place on floured surface to dry. I use my kitchen table. I place a tablecloth on it and dry all the sheets of dough on it adding flour on top and bottom of sheets. Dry the sheets for about 30 minutes then on the smallest opening cut the sheets forming thin like spaghetti. Place on floured platter until you are ready to cook. In a large pot of boiling salted water add the fresh fagiolini and bring to boil for about 5 minutes. Drain completely and add to chicken broth (recipe in the book).

If you don't have a pasta machine, divide the dough in three and with wooden rolling pin roll three equal thin circles and dry on floured board for 30 minutes. Then roll into jelly like rolls and cut thin noodles with sharp knife.

SPAGHETTI CON VONGOLE

Spaghetti with Clams

2 Dozen small clams the size of a quarter (most fish markets will have them)
Wash and rinse well, use only closed clams
1/4 cup extra virgin olive oil
2 cloves chopped garlic
1 small bunch of fresh parsley (coarsely chopped)

2-4 leaves fresh basil (or 1/2 teaspoon of dried)
1-teaspoon kosher salt
1/4 teaspoon dried pepper flakes (optional)
1 lb. Spaghetti
1 cup peeled and chopped tomatoes
4 ounces tomato sauce
3 tablespoon white wine or 3 tablespoon of water

In a medium size pot, place oil and garlic and lightly brown, add clams and wine. Toss lightly then add chopped tomatoes, tomato sauce, parsley, basil, salt and pepper flakes. Reduce heat to low and simmer for 15-20 minutes. Taste and add more salt if necessary.

Meanwhile boil a large pot of water add 1 tablespoon of kosher salt and cook 1 lb. of spaghetti a dente. Drain well, return to pot and add half of the prepared clam sauce. Toss lightly and serve adding a ladle of sauce with clams on each plate. Eat the clams and discard shells. Serves 4-6 people

SPAGHETTI CON GAMBERI

Spaghetti with shrimp

1 lb spaghetti
1 lb large shrimp, shelled and cleaned
1/4 cup white wine
1/4 cup extra virgin olive oil
1 small bunch fresh parley (coarsely chopped
1-teaspoon kosher salt
black pepper for garnish
2 cloves chopped garlic

In a medium saucepan add oil, garlic and lightly brown. Now add shrimp and salt, and then add wine, and parsley. Turn heat to low and cook for an additional 10 minutes.

Meanwhile boil a large pot of water, add salt and cook spaghetti a dente. Drain well and return to pot, and then add half the shrimp sauce. Serve up each plate then add a little extra reserved shrimp sauce. Fresh pepper can be added to each plate. Serves 4-6 people

RICE,
POTATOES
AND
POLENTA

4

RISOTTO

1 lb Arborio rice
1/4 cup dried porcini mushrooms (finely chopped) button mushrooms can be substituted.
2-tablespoon Parmesan cheese or more
1-2 quarts chicken or vegetable stocks (add saffron and allow to simmer)
2-tablespoon extra virgin olive oil
1 package saffron or 1/2 teaspoon dried saffron
Salt and pepper to taste
One medium onion (finely chopped)
1/4 cup dry white wine

In a large skillet or stockpot place oil and onion sauté for about 5 minutes add porcini or mushrooms. (Soak dried porcini for 30 minutes in a bowl of warm water to soften) add to skillet and save the liquid for later.

Add rice, stir and coat with oil in the pot. Now add wine and continue to cook on medium heat for a couple more minutes. Begin adding stock to rice one cup at the time. When the liquid is absorbed add more stock. Carefully add reserved poricini liquid to stock. Cook the rice for about 20 minuets or until risotto is al dente (to the tooth) turn off the stove and add the Parmesan cheese and serve. Extra cheese can be added to each serving plate. Serve immediately. It will nice and creamy...
Makes 4-6 serving.

PIZZA DI GRANDURCO

Fried Corn Pizza

3 quarts of water
1-tablespoon kosher salt
3 tablespoons of extra virgin olive oil
1 cup of cornmeal

In cold water, add salt and one tablespoon of oil. Now, with Wisk add the cornmeal the water mixture. Continue to stir with wooded spoon occasionally. When the cornmeal comes together and thickens remove from the heat and set aside. In a medium non-stick pan add the two tablespoons of oil, Flatten the cornmeal in the pan. It should be about 1/2 inch thick. Cook on the stove medium heat until crispy. Now, turn and cook other side. Place a large plate over the pan and invert and slide uncooked side down. Continue cooking on other side for a few more minutes. Serve cooked fried corn polenta pizza in wedges with escarole and beans.

POLENTA

3 cups of water
2 Tablespoon extra virgin olive oil
1 Tablespoon kosher salt
1 Cups of cornmeal (course or fine can be used)
Parmesan cheese
1 basic tomato sauce recipe

In a large pot place water, oil, salt and cornmeal. Now with Wisk add in the cornmeal all at once. Now on medium heat with a wooden spoon stir as the polenta absorbed the water and cooks. This can take five to ten minutes. Do not leave it. A little more water can be added if necessary. Once you have achieved the right texture. Transfer to platter or in individual dish... Keep adding cornmeal until you have reached a smooth consistency. Transfer to serving plate. Individual plates are served with a ladle of hot tomato sauce and a sprinkle of Parmesan cheese.

This polenta can be served with many chicken dishes. Leftover polenta fried in a pan with olive oil is great.

INSALATA DI PATATE

Italian Potato Salad

6-8 medium to large potatoes
2 stalks of celery
1 medium onion red or regular
2 cucumbers
3-4 plum tomatoes (do not use very ripened tomatoes hard and crunchy are better)
1/4 cup extra virgin olive oil
1-2 teaspoon kosher Salt,
1 clove of chopped garlic
1 teaspoon dried oregano

2-3 leaves of fresh basil if available
1/2 cup of your favorite olives

Wash the potatoes, leaving the skin on. place in a pot of cold water and cook until tender. Use a fork to test.

Drain and cool potatoes

Peel potatoes and cut in cube size

Cut all remaining vegetable in bite size, add garlic, basil and oregano. Add salt to taste, add oil and toss. Serve at room temperature.

Taste and adjust seasoning
Server's 6-8 people

PATATE IMBOTTITE

Twice Stuffed Potatoes

4-6 baking potatoes
1 egg
2-tablespoon Parmesan cheese
1/4 cup of cubed mozzarella cheese
1 tablespoon of fresh parsley
Salt and pepper to taste
2 tablespoons of extra virgin olive oil. Bake potatoes until done. Slice lengthwise, scoop the cavity without disturbing the skin, Place scooped potatoes in a bowl add all the above ingredients and mix well. (Reserve 1 tablespoon of parmesan cheese for later use) refill potatoes.

Place olive oil in a shallow baking dish; place filled potatoes and sprinkle 1 tablespoon of Parmesan cheese

Rebake for 15 minutes at 350, broil for 2-3 additional minutes.

FRITTATA

Growing up frittata was always served on Fridays a non-meat eating day. I remember potato frittata, zucchini frittata, onion or asparagus frittata was served as our second course with homemade bread my mother made in her brick oven outdoor near the kitchen. The leftovers were great for sandwiches the next day. The most favorite was the potato frittata. The recipe can be substituted with other vegetables or left over spaghetti. Follow the same recipe for any other frittata

FRITTATA DI PATATE

Potato Frittata

4 medium all purpose potatoes
2 tablespoon of Parmesan cheese
1/4 cup extra virgin olive oil
2 tsps of kosher salt
4 extra large eggs
1/4 teaspoon of black pepper

———

Peel, wash and towel dry the potatoes. Cut into small cubes. Place in heated oiled non-stick pan. Cook on medium heat until light brown or tender; add one teaspoon of salt.

In a separate bowl, beat eggs, pepper, cheese and 1 teaspoon of salt. Mix well with a fork and pour over cooked potatoes. With a fork carefully pinch to allow the eggs to run and cook well. Cook for 5-10 on low. Turning the frittata is a real challenge, cover the skillet with a large platter and then flip the pan over so that the frittata lands bottom side up on the plate, now slide the frittata with side down back into the skillet. Cook until the second side is also golden. I turn the frittata over the sink, just in case, but I have always been successful. Good luck.

CROQUETTE DI PATATE

Potato Croquettes

6-8 medium all purpose potatoes
3 Eggs
1/4 cup of grated Parmesan cheese
1 1/2 teaspoon kosher salt
1 teaspoon of black pepper

1/4 cup flavored breadcrumbs
2 cups of vegetable oil (for frying)

Place washed unpeeled potatoes in a large pot, fill with cold water until the potatoes are covered. Bring to boil and reduce heat. Cook until tender. Test doness with fork. Drain and cool slightly. Peel immediately and squeeze thru a potato ricer. Cool potatoes a little more, then add eggs, cheese, salt and pepper and breadcrumbs. Mix gently. Form with your hand 2 inch logs about 1/2 inch thick. Place potato crockets in hot oil. Turn only once when golden brown. Remove from hot oil and drain on paper towels. During the shaping process you will need to wash your hands periodically. Wet your hand with a little water, it will make shaping a lot easier. Shape all the croquettes and place on a platter before frying. Serve them hot. Make approximately 20 crockets.

PATATE ARROSTITE

Pan Roasted Potatoes

6 Medium size potatoes
1 teaspoon dried oregano
1-teaspoon kosher salt
1/2 teaspoon black pepper
2-tablespoon Parmesan cheese
3 tablespoon of extra virgin olive oil

Peel and wash and dry with paper towel (peeling the potatoes is optional). Slice potatoes 1/4 inch thick forming circles. In roasting pan place a tablespoon of extra virgin olive oil and line the roasting pan forming one layer. Drizzle the rest of the oil over the potatoes. Now sprinkle the rest of the ingredients and place in a preheated 375-degree oven for 45 minutes to 1 hour or until crispy and golden. Remove and transfer to

DESSERTS
AND
TREATS

5

PIZZA RUSTICA

Easter sausage and Prosciutto Pie

1 Basic crust for top and bottom (see recipe)
1 10x3 deep dish pie pan or spring form pan approximately the same size
8 large eggs
1-2 lbs fresh cheese (specialty markets carry this at Easter time)
1/2 cup pecorino Romano cheese
1-2 dry sweet sausage cubed
1/2 lbs of prosciutto (buy it in one piece then slices it yourself into 2-inch strips 1/4 inch tick
    and cube
Tablespoon black pepper
1 tablespoon vegetable shortening

In a mixing bowl, beat eggs, black pepper, pecorino cheese and fresh cheese (crumble sliced fresh cheese in the egg mixture.
Add the sliced prosciutto and sausage to the egg mixture.
In a well-greased deep pie pan place crust overlapping on the edge, pour all the egg mixture with prosciutto and sausage into it. Place second crust over the pan. With bottom overlapped crust roll into top crust. Form a rolled edge. With a fork press top and bottom crust to seal. Use a little shortening around the rimmed crust to keep moist while baking. Also with fork prick the top of fork to prevent the crust to swell. Place the pie into a 350-degree oven for 1 hour until golden brown. Cover with a piece of aluminum foil if the crust is getting too dark too quick. The pie must cook for the entire hour. Cool in oven. Remove and cool completely. Refrigerate overnight. Eat it cold or room temperature.

BASIC CRUST #1

2-3 Cups of flour
1 Tablespoon Pecorino Romano cheese
1-Teaspoon Pepper
1 Tablespoon of Vegetable Shortening
1/4 Cup cold water

In a mixing bowl place 2 cups of flour, cheese, pepper and crisco add in half of the water and mix. Add more flour and water until it forms a ball. Transfer to a board and cover. Divide into 2 balls. Flour the board and roll one crust slightly bigger than pie dish. Repeat for the top crust, but make the crust slightly smaller.

BASIC CRUST #2

1 sticks butter room temperature
1 large egg
1-teaspoon baking powder
Pinch salt
2 or more cups flour
Iced water

Place butter, flour salt and baking power in food processor with blade... Pulse until pea consistency. Now add egg and ice water. Mix until you form a soft ball. Do not over mix. Refrigerate for 1 hour. Divide the dough in half and roll on floured surface when you are ready for the pie.

BISCOTTI
Hazelnuts and chocolate

2 1/2 cups unbleached flour
3/4 cup sugar

1 tsp vanilla extract
Pinch salt
3 eggs
1 tsp baking powder
 1/2 tsp baking soda
1/2 cup lightly roasted hazelnuts
1/2 cup chopped dark chocolate
2 tablespoon of milk (for glazing)

Mix together eggs, sugar, vanilla adds dry ingredients. Then mix will be course and mealy, add nuts and chocolate. Transfer to a board and form two logs about 10 in long. Place in a greased cookie sheet; flatten the top a little with your hands. Brush milk over the logs. Bake 350 degrees for 30 minutes. Remove from oven. Slice the biscotti with a bread knife replace into cookie sheet and place in the over. Turn oven off. Leave for two hours or longer. Store in a covered plastic container and refrigerate.
Makes approx 24 biscotti

TORTA DI BANANA

Banana Bread

4 Large ripened bananas
3 eggs
1-cup sugar
1 tsp vanilla
1/2 cup vegetable oil
1 3/4 cups flour
Pinch salt
1 tsp baking soda
1/2 tsp baking powder
1 cup chopped walnuts (optional)

Mix ingredients in listed order
Makes 4 mini loaves or 1 large loaf (please grease pans)
Bake 350 for 1 hour.

ZIA MEMES BISCOTTI

Walnut mini tarts

—Dough
2 sticks butter (room temp)
6 oz cream cheese (room temp)
16 oz flour

———————

Mix together and refrigerate for 1 hour

Use 4 mini muffin pans. Each pan holds 12 mini muffins

—Filling
2 eggs
12 oz light brown sugar
12 oz chopped walnuts
 1 tablespoon melted butter
1-tablespoon vanilla extract
1 pinch salt

———————

Mix above ingredients set aside. With the refrigerated dough form 72 golf size balls and mould each into mini muffin pans using your fingers or a wooden tool (especially made for this process)

Spoon mixture about three fourth of the way. Do not overfill.

Bake at 350 degrees for approximately 20 minutes
or until lightly golden
Makes 72 tarts
Remove immediately and place on a cool rack
Sprinkle with confection sugar

PASTIERA NAPOLETANA

Easter Grain Pie

Pastry for pie
Pasta Frolla
3 cups unbleached flour
2 eggs
1/2 cups sugar
1/4 cup butter (room temperature)
1-teaspoon vanilla
1 pinch salt
1 tsp baking powder
1-tablespoon milk

Mix together in a food processor or by hand, form into a ball wrap In saran wrap and refrigerate for about 1 hour.

—For the filling
6 large eggs
3/4 cup sugar
Zest of one orange and zest one lemon
1/4 cup citron (can be bought in a specialty store at Easter time)
1 lb ricotta (Put in a strainer overnight to remove excess water)
8 ounce cooked wheat (it can be bought cooked in a can)
1-cup milk
1 pinch salt

Warm milk in a pan adds cooked wheat for about 5 min on medium, set aside. With an electric mix, beat egg yolks, sugar ricotta, and add the cooked wheat mixture and the rest of the ingredients, set aside. Mix egg whites in a separate bowl to form a peak, fold in the mixture and set aside.

Roll pastry into 2 equal circles about 9-10-pie size. Place in pie dish add the mixture. For the top cut strips about 1/2 with pastry wheel and form a lattice overlapping on the sides. Cut and with a fork press down all around the pie. Brush the top with a little milk. Place in 350 degree pre heated over on a cookie sheet (in case of spills) cook for about 1 hour or until top of pie is golden brown. Cool and refrigerate overnight before serving. Dust with powder sugar and serve.

TIRAMISU

1 Package lady fingers (16 oz)
16. Oz mascarpone cheese
8 oz. whipping cream
1 large pot espresso coffee (mixed in 3 tablespoon sugar while hot, mix and set aside)
Additional 4-tablespoon sugar
1/4cup of any coffee flavored liquor
1/4 cup of dark cocoa powder
9-inch spring form pan (the kind used for cheesecakes)

In a mixing bowl mix mascarpone cheese and 3 tablespoon of sugar mix well, now add ½ of liquor, mix and set aside. . Whip the whipping cream and fold into the mascarpone mixture.

Now add the rest of the liquor to the coffee and sugar mixture.

Dip the ladyfingers one at a time in the coffee liquid and line bottom of pan. Spread 1/3 of the mascarpone; continue with dipped ladyfingers until you have three layers of each.

The last layer should be the mascarpone mixture. With a strainer sift the cocoa powder on the top. Place in freezer overnight or longer... Place in the refrigerator in the morning of the night you are planning to serve.

Makes 8-10 servings.

TORTA DI MELA

Apple Pie

2 Basic oversized crust #2 (see recipe in the book)

—*Filling*
6-8 large apples (use a mixed variety like Granny Smith, Gala, Empire and Macintosh)
2 Teaspoon cinnamon
1/4 teaspoon cloves
1/2 cup sugar (plus one tablespoon for top)
2-tablespoon flour
Small grating nutmeg

1 Tablespoon lemon juice
2 Tablespoon of butter cut into small pieces
2-tablespoon milk for glazing

Peel and slice apples. Place in a bowl add all the ingredients for filling. Cover and allow macerating for 15 minutes.

In a deep 10-inch pie dish place one basic oversized crust. Place the apples into the crust. Now add one more crust over the pie dish. Put a little water on the rim of the bottom crust. This will allow the top crust to seal well. Now with a fork or your fingers finish the piecrust. Brush the pie with a little milk, then sprinkle with a tablespoon of sugar place a cookie sheet while baking to prevent overspill in your oven. Remove and cool completely before serving.

TORTA CON ZUCCA DOLCE

Thanksgiving butternut Pie

1 large butternut squash
1-cup sugar
1-pint heavy cream
6 eggs
1/2 teaspoon allspice
1-teaspoon cinnamon
¼ tsp. grated nutmeg
1-teaspoon vanilla
1 basic crust

The day before, wash and slice the butternut squash lengthwise, remove seeds and bake in a 350-degree oven in a pan with 1/4 cup of water. Remove; peel the skin and puree.

Combine pureed squash, with sugar, vanilla and eggs and mix well with electric mixer. Add in spices and almost all the heavy cream. (Reserve 2 ounce to whip to garnish). Line a 10-inch deep pie pan and pour into it. Bake for 1 hour at 350 degree. This recipe makes 2 small 9-inch pies or 1 deep-dish 10-inch pie. Remove from the oven and cool. Transfer to refrigerate and chill. Whip the reserved heavy cream and garnish in small quarter size on top of pie.

CRANBERRY SAUCE

1 16oz. Bag of fresh cranberries
1-cup sugar
1-cup water
1 orange with skin, chopped in a food process

Wash cranberries and place in a deep saucepan. Add sugar water and chopped orange. Cook on medium heat until all the cranberries pop. The mixture gets a preserve consistency. Cook for 20 minutes. Transfer to a glass or ceramic dish and chill.

BRENNOLE

Tarallini with Pepper and Fennel

1 Cup of olive oil
1 Cup of white wine
1 Cup of cold water
2 Tablespoon kosher salt sea salt
1 Tablespoon black pepper (more if you prefer)
1 Tablespoon dried fennel seeds
4-5 Cups unbleached flour (more may be necessary)
1-tablespoon baking powder

In a large bowl place oil, wine, water, salt, pepper and fennel seeds. Mix in 1 cup of flour adding in the baking powder. Continue to mix with a wooden spoon. Keep adding the flour until the mixture is forming into a softball. It can also be mixed by hand (which we do) stop adding in the flour when your hand is clean and the mixture is not sticking to your hand. Transfer the mixture to a wooden board. Knead for a couple of minutes. Flour the board, so the mixture does not stick. Keep dough on the side, cover with clean cloth. On the same wooden board take little pieces of the dough and roll into twelve-inch logs approximately half inch thick. Close the log by pinches both sides forming a circle. Place on cookie sheets. The sheets need not be greased. Bake oven 375 for 30-45 min or until golden brown.

BISCOTTI DI PISTACCHI

Cranberry Pistachio Biscotti

2 1/2 cups unbleached flour
1-cup sugar
3 eggs
1/2 teaspoon baking powder
1/2 teaspoon baking soda
1 pinch of salt
1 teaspoon of pure vanilla extract
1 cup dried cranberries (soak in warm water for 10 minutes)
1 cup unsalted raw pistachios

In a mixing bowl place sugar, eggs, vanilla and mix well add the flour, salt, baking power and baking soda and mix. Add pistachios and drained soaked cranberries. Transfer to a floured board and form two equal logs the length of a large cookie sheet. Place on greased cookies sheet and flatten with your palm. Brush with either egg white or milk. Bake at 350 degree preheated oven for 25 minutes. Remove and slice with bread knife 1/4 inch thick. Return to cookie sheet and bake for an additional 10 minutes. Turn off the oven and leave for 1 hour or overnight. Makes about 4 dozens

STRUFFOLI

Honey Balls

3 eggs
 1-teaspoon baking powder
2-3 cups unbleached flour
2-tablespoon vegetable oil
2-tablespoon anisette liquor (optional)
1 teaspoon of vanilla extract
2-tablespoon sugar
1quart of vegetable oil (for frying)
1-2 tablespoon colored round sprinkles for decoration

In a mixer combine eggs, vanilla or anisette, sugar and oil. Add flour 1 cup at a time with baking powder. Keep adding the flour a little at a time until a ball forms and does not stick to your hands. Remove from bowl and kneed on lightly floured surface for a couple of minutes. Cover and set aside.

On a lightly floured surface pinch a little dough and roll into 12 inch long 1/4 inch thick. With sharp knife cut each struffoli 1/4 inch in size. Continue with the remainder of dough. Place cut struffoli on a floured dish or platter to avoid sticking. Meanwhile in a large stock pot place 4 inches of vegetable oil and heat. As the oil heats place one struffoli in it, when it starts to bubble you know the oil is hot enough to begin cooking the rest. Add one salad plate full of uncooked struffoli to oil each time. Stir with wooden spoon and cook on medium heat. Cook until golden, and then remove with slotted spoon and place on paper towel to drain. Continue until all the uncooked struffoli are done. More oil can be added to pot if necessary, but keep the oil level no more than 4 inch in the pot to avoid spillage and burn. A basket frying can be used but use caution whenever you fry.

HONEY GLAZE FOR STRUFFOLI

16 oz the best honey
4 tablespoon of sugar
1-tablespoon water

In a large pot place honey and sugar. On medium heat dissolve and cook until it comes to a steady boil. Continue to cook on low for about 5 more minutes or until it starts to slightly thicken. Remove from heat and pour over the cooked struffoli in a large mixing bowl. Stir and coat the entire batch. Transfer to a serving dish sprinkle with colored sprinkles and cover with plastic wrap. They keep for days. Serve room temperature. Do not refrigerate.

ROSETTE (ZIA ANNETTELLA)

3 Eggs
3 Teaspoon of distilled white vinegar
3 Tablespoon of sugar
Juice of one lemon
1 Teaspoon of baking powder
Flour (3-4 cups it varies)

1 Tablespoon of anisette liquor

2 or more cups of vegetable oil

1 tablespoon of powdered sugar for garnish

1 cup of amarena (tart cherry preserve) recipe in the book, your favorite preserve can be substituted

1 cup of custard (recipe in the book) optional

2 inch round cookie cutter and 3 inch round cookie cutter (*we use drinking glass, one larger than the other.*)

In a large mixing bowl with wooden spoon, cream eggs, sugar, lemon juice, vinegar and liquor. One cup at a time add flour and baking powder. Mix by hand adding more flour until the mixture forms a ball and your hand no longer sticks. Transfer to a board and cover with wrap. With a rolling pin, roll 1/3 of the dough. Form a small ball, flour the board and roll the dough very thin. With the cookie cutter, cut equal amounts of circles with both size cutters. Dip in clean flour to cut easier. Score with a knife each circle at 12-o clock at 3, at 6 and 9 o'clock from the outside in half way to the center. Place small scored circle on top of the larger scored circle pressing the center with your finger down. Continue until you run out of dough. As you are cutting and rolling place the prepared cookies on a floured tray before frying.

Heat a deep skillet with 2-3 cups of vegetable oil. The oil should be 2-3 inches deep and very hot. Drop in the prepared cookies and cook until golden brown. Drain on paper towel. Repeat until all done. The heat can be reduced to medium if you feel necessary. It takes approximately 2-3 minutes to cook.

Cool the cooked cookie. Spoon on 1 teaspoon of custard and 1 teaspoon of preserve over the custard. Powder with confection sugar and serve.

AMARENA

Cherry Preserve

This is a specialty from our region of Italy. In late June these very tart cherries are picked and pitted. Cooked with sugar in a large pot over low heat. Simmering for hours until done. As small children we would help my mother and grandmother pit baskets and baskets of these very tart cherries. It would take hours to do this by hand. Our clothes would be painted by all the splattered juice that would come out from the pitting process. Today women including my mother still follow the same process to make this special preserve. After it is cooked and prepared according to the recipe. It is placed in small glass jars. Cleaned sterilized jars are used. Emptied jars from other foods are saved and used for this process. The jarred preserve is stored with the closed lids in room temperature or in the cantina (cool cellar) this preserve is used to put on many desserts and ice cream. My mother still sends from Italy jars of this amarena for our consumption here in the States. We have not attempted to make this here in America. So if you are lucky enough to visit Italy, this preserve can be purchased in my grocery stores. It is commonly used in the Campania region in Italy. Places like Naples and many other places in the South of Italy.

Here is the recipe according to my mother. Other cherries can be substituted to achieve similar results.

1 Kilogram of tart pitted cherries
350 grams of sugar

———

Place in a deep saucepan and cook slowly for 30 minutes. Stir occasionally to prevent sticking. Lower the heat and continue cooking until it thickens. Transfer to a platter and allow it to cool. When it is completely cooled, place in clean sterilized glass jar and store in a cool place or refrigerate. It stores indefinitely.

CHEESECAKE

3- 8 oz package cream cheese
4 large eggs
1 1/4 cup sugar
1-tablespoon pure vanilla extract
8 oz sour cream

—Crust
1 cup of grounded graham crackers
2 tablespoon melted butter
1 10-inch cheesecake pan

———

Mix the graham cracker crumbs and butter. Line the bottom of cheesecake pan and bake for 10 minutes.

With an electric mixer, cream the cream cheese, add sugar and vanilla. Then add sour cream and one egg continue mixing until all the eggs are incorporated. Pour into the prepared pan with graham. Cook the cheesecake in a water bath. You can do this by pouring 1 inch of boiling water in a pan larger than the cheesecake pan. Place the uncooked cheesecake into the larger pan and bake at 350 degree for 1 hour.

Reduce the oven to 325 degree and continue baking for an additional 45 min.

Turn off the oven and cool completely in the oven. With door open. When it is completely cool, place on a serving platter and refrigerate for at least 4 hours or longer before serving. Garnish with your favorite fruits and powdered sugar.

BISCOTTI DI CIOCCOLATO

Cathryn's chocolate chip cookies

!/3 cup butter
1/3 cup vegetable shortening
1-teaspoon vanilla extract
1/2 cup white sugar
½ cup brown sugar
1 egg
1-½ cups flour
½ teaspoon baking soda
½ teaspoon salt
¾ cup semisweet chocolate chips

Oven 375 degrees
Mix sugar, butter, shortening, egg and vanilla (room temperature)
Add vanilla
Stir in flour, baking soda, and salt. Add chips
Drop dough with tablespoon two inches apart
Bake until light brown. (8-10 minutes)

CROSTATA DI FRUTTA

Fruit tart

Piecrust for tart
1-cup flour
½ butter
1 teaspoon orange zest
Pinch of salt

――――

4 oz. mascarpone cheese
¼ cup sugar
1 pint strawberries, washes and sliced
¼ cup raspberries
¼ cup blueberries
3 kiwis peeled and sliced
1 small jar apricot jams for glaze

――――

Combine room temperature butter, flour, salt and orange zest. In a food process until it comes together. With your hands spread evenly in a tart pan. Bake at 350 for 10-15 minutes. Remove and cool.

Now mix room temperature mascarpone and sugar spread evenly on cooled tart. Now arrange fruit starting with the strawberries.
In a small saucepan heat the apricot jam until loosened. Cool
Spoon over fruit

ABOUT THE AUTHOR

Elizabeth Iadevaia, was born in Durazzano, a small town north of Naples, Italy. She immigrated to the United States with her parents, two brothers and one sister, at the age of twelve. She currently lives in Commack, Long Island with her son Vincent and daughter Cathryn. This is her first cookbook. A collection of old favorite recipes inspired by her mother and grandmother, and some new ones she's collected over the years